# TERES

# TERESA OF AVILA

**Kate O'Brien**

**MERCIER PRESS**

**Mercier Press**
PO Box 5, 5 French Church Street, Cork
24 Lower Abbey Street, Dublin 1

© Kate O'Brien 1951

ISBN 1 85635 054 1

First published in 1951 and reprinted in 1967.
This edition 1993

*Cover design by John Skelton, from statue of Saint Teresa by Bernini in church of Santa Maria Della Vittoria in Rome.*

Printed in Ireland by Colour Books Ltd.

# CONTENTS

I    Introduction . . . . . . . . . . . . . . 9

II    Childhood . . . . . . . . . . . . . . . 16

III    Vocation . . . . . . . . . . . . . . . . 28

IV    'Martha and Mary walking about together'    62

# ACKNOWLEDGMENTS

The author's thanks are due to Professor E. Allison Peers for permission to quote from his translations of Saint Teresa's *Spiritual Relations*, *The Way of Perfection* and *The Interior Castle*.

*Chapter One*

# INTRODUCTION

Let no reader suppose that in the few pages here set before him he will find either the life or, miraculously trapped, the spirit of Teresa of Avila. The present attempt is a portrait, or rather, it is notes for a portrait; it is an apology not for Teresa but for this writer's constant admiration of her.

Teresa's mortal life, the vessel which contained her, withheld a residue when her flame had left it. This residue is a dust very rich in unusual elements. But to build back with it to what it was four hundred years ago, when the life of a human soul informed it, can only be impressionistic work. Since therefore all statement, all surmise set out henceforward here will be quite sincerely arbitrary, that is to say, freely developed from one writer's long reflection on a markedly individual and dangerous fellow creature, it will be best if that writer pass without delay from the third to the first person singular.

I write of Teresa of Avila by choice which is passionate, arbitrary, personal. No one need agree with anything I have to say – but they must not, either, be hurt thereby. I am free to speak freely about a great woman. But I am not writing of the canonized saint. I propose to examine Teresa, not by the rules of canonization, but for what she was – saint or not – a woman of genius.

Women of genius are few. If there have been some female stars in science, medicine or the plastic arts, I must be forgiven if I ignore them here, where I pursue only the idea of genius expressed in the word, and in action arising from the power of the word. Reducing then, for purposes of convenience, our discussion of genius in woman to her power in and because of words – which is the most probable way for the expressive to reach the inexpressive – and searching for examples of it we find very few.

We know or can argue the reasons – but there is not space to dispute them here. That dying Europe is thick incrustated with the glories of male intelligence and may presently vanish before woman has had time or chance to make her possible impression on a superb, doomed effort – that is clear enough. But, before catastrophe cracks in all our dreaming faces, let us enumerate our precious things and people. Let us say our personal says. I say, with great regret, that within the two thousand or so years that my very poorly trained vision can take in, genius has hardly ever flowered in a woman. We can jump back beyond those two thousand years and boast of Sappho. But we have only fragments, rumours of her – and in any case we have to wait for a woman to match her until England and the nineteenth century. It is strange; all the variable, definable furies, styles and freedoms could pass over Europe – we could have Virgil, Lucretius, Dante, Ronsard, Shakespeare, Racine, Madame de La Fayette and Miss Jane Austen – but there was still no tracking down of a *woman* who could be called genius until Emily Brontë's burning shadow flung out. Not as broken, not as indefinable as Sappho's, but strangely sympathetic to her legend, and just as unsatisfactory. And they are the only female geniuses of our recorded knowledge in literature.

But, for our consolation, there have been women who, had they not been too large and too much perplexed by the old dilemma of being women, might have been almost as immeasurably great. However, the trouble about genius, if we must define it – and here, in relation to Teresa of Avila, we must try to – is that there must be no 'almost' about its quality. Sappho and Emily Brontë were both lucky in the shortness and the veiledness of their lives. We know nothing about either of them – and each has been able to inform us nevertheless of her immortality. That is wonderful – that is, in fact, what it is to be a great poet.

Now we must face my complicated exception Teresa of Avila was *not* a great poet. But she was a formidable writer of prose. Indeed, in certain difficult passages of expression, passages luminously, miraculously great, as I shall try to show, we hear a great poet, who had to be used in another field of genius. Even so, her prose, for all its marvellous accidental beauties, does not, *qua* writing, entitle her to be called 'genius'. Any more than would the writings of Catherina of Siena, brilliant as they were, entitle her to the word genius in literature. But these two women were geniuses in their lives – and our only reason for being sure of that is that we can read their records, their thoughts, their reasons; we can get their *apologiae* for their extraordinary conduct of life from their own vibrating words. Teresa, who could have been, was a literary genius, was in fact a woman of genius who had other than literary business, and who used words, which were indeed her easy slaves, only for purposes which had nothing to do with literature, but solely with God. (God, if I may say so without disrespect, was very lucky in His random, witty, gifted Teresa.)

My claim therefore for Teresa as a woman of genius – which is only the claim of centuries of the learned – is not that she was a *writer* of genius, in the pure sense of Sappho and Emily Brontë, but that her brilliant and sometimes transcendentally marvellous writing – granted all its impatience and carelessness – has left us the record of life lived by a genius. Wherefore I claim for her that through the power of the word – since her words have left us what she was – Teresa was a woman of genius. On lonely terms, her own. A minor poet; an easy, fluent, careless writer of prose, who, compelled again and again by high necessity, could say in plain words – because she had to – what greater writers could never say. That is why literature must half-accept, and life – life wherein we seek for God – must wholly embrace Teresa as a genius.

She was *expressive* – peculiarly endowed to express. Whatever she wrote – that rang, that rings and stays, and builds about it great suggestions. Her prose has a simple 'clang' in it which is indeed Castilian.

One cannot say that her easy, living Castilian equals in grace the beautiful, easy French of Madame de Sévigné, though admittedly she used it with triumphant naturalness to interpret experiences entirely beyond the imaginative scope of the seventeenth-century marquise; and it is as true that her quill could not match in precision the one that Jane Austen sharpened as that the lady of the English parsonage would have turned with a shudder of distaste from many of the searching, strange records set down by the Carmelite nun. But the Carmelite nun was a personality much larger than normal life, which neither of these other two delightful writers was; and it is because she was able to establish that personality for ever in many enchantingly readable prose works, and in her letters, that we know wherein her genius lay. It was a genius for life; Teresa lived as a genius.

This may be only one way of saying that she lived several lives, and lived each one intensely and to its fullest exaction; she passed from plane to plane of human experience, always alert, always with all her mighty wits about her. She dreamt, she aspired, she laughed, romanticized and sinned; she suffered, both in body and spirit, as few can have done; she observed, she studied; she directed human destinies; she mastered and ruled the intractable stuff of external life; she explored, accurately and modestly, the dangerous regions of her own rare spirit and founded therein her 'interior castle'; she 'saw' God – and struggled scrupulously to interpret that 'seeing' to us; she became, by the combined and constant experience of self-discipline, modesty, courage and wit, the least pretentious, the most approachable and the most tranquil of Christian mystics. And the story of all this victory she left behind her in writings as honest and natural as they are beautiful. She wrote only for practical purposes, for the furtherance in this way or that of her reform; but in so doing she accidentally wrote the testament of a genius. Because of her gift of clear expressiveness her stormy and tormented human life shines now across human history as the 'way of perfection' into which she shaped it.

*Chapter Two*

# CHILDHOOD

Teresa de Cepeda y Ahumada was born in the Castilian town of Avila in 1515, the year in which Martin Luther formulated his dogma of grace. For anyone in any century, to be born and to be a child in Avila is a stroke of luck, and Teresa and her birthplace were undoubtedly sympathetic to each other. Avilans say, with a shrug, that when Christ was a child by the Sea of Galilee their town was more or less as it is now, and if this claim is not examined too literally, the truth it intends may be allowed. Its famous walls came round the city indeed as late as the end of the eleventh century A.D., and somewhat later the dark and angry fortress-Cathedral grew into their shadow; and with the passing ages those things which a town raises and discards passed in and out of life in Avila – churches, palaces and inns, tombs and hermitages, escutcheons, cloisters, fountains, holy relics; hotels and trains; motor-coaches, cafés and loud-speakers; electric light, and running water hot and cold – all these expressions of man's passage wash, as always they have washed, in and out of Avila, some hardly noticeable, some staying to live and die with the town, some seeking, vainly, to remake it. But the Avilans themselves are probably right in feeling that the place has not really changed very much since its citizens received St. Peter's deacon from Rome in the year 63, and heard the first of the Christian message.

Yet the Christian message was to bring to the Castilian and local character at least as much as that character was to impose upon it. Indeed one might say that in the meeting of these two forces, destined so irresistibly to interlock, was born the spirit of Avila. And Teresa, late, strong flower of that spirit, came into life at an hour when the civilized world – in which Spain, Castilian Spain, played a leading part – was about to submit to a tidal wave of change. The Renaissance was aflood in Europe at her birth, the Reformation was gathering up on a curve of coming power, and the Middle Ages were already adrift along the past, in dark recession. The girl-baby, who was christened Teresa after her maternal grandmother on 4th April 1515 at the font of the eleventh-century church of St. John, was to grow up to apprehend all that as few are able to apprehend their contemporary scene; to apprehend first – and afterwards to take action, to lead in defence of man's 'interior castle', and in the salvaging of certain rigours, disciplines and principles which her brilliant century was impassioned to sweep away.

But that was only a part of what Teresa was to do, and learn to do.

Both houses of her family held patents of nobility. Her father was an impoverished and, probably, a somewhat helpless *hidalgo*; he appears to have been proud, pious, affectionate, and lacking in initiative; her mother, Doña Beatriz Ahumada, was Don Alonso's second wife; she was wealthy, owning farms and house property around Avila. She is said to have had beauty, and, as all the world knows, she was a great reader of novels and passed on this vice to her daughter Teresa. But marriage and the bearing of many children invalided her, and she died, seeming much older than her years, when she was thirty-three and Teresa thirteen.

Neither of these parents, in the little tradition tells us of them, offers any clue to the personality of their elder daughter. Nor does that daughter in her childhood reflect the woman she was to be. She came in the middle of a regiment of brothers, and it is clear that in her games and pursuits these brothers either did as she directed or she dispensed with their companionship and played alone. She was a highly imaginative and inquiring child; also, I surmise, she was bossy and an organizer. We know from her autobiography that she was cunning and subtle and could keep her own business to herself. But these are characteristics of practically all intelligent children. The famous episode of her setting off when she was six to seek martyrdom from the Moors and being brought home when a mile out of town by an uncle who happened to ride past her is the entertaining kind of story told of many children. She took her brother Rodrigo with her on that expedition, and the fact that Rodrigo, who was ten – four years older than Teresa – blamed the whole escapade on her and was believed shows her clearly in her character of ringleader. (True enough, she was always to be that – in everything she put her hand to she became ringleader.) But she tells us herself that her baby plan to get martyred was no more than a cunning device to secure eternal happiness cheaply. She had been considering eternity and the eternal horrors of hell; the latter prospect terrified her, and as she knew that Christian martyrdom guaranteed instant admission to everlasting glory, she thought, and explained to Rodrigo, that the clever thing to do was to get martyred while martyrdom was possible. It is a plan which might have occurred to any vividly-minded child of any over-pious Catholic household.

So also with her games of 'monasterio' and of 'Prioress', and with the 'hermitages' which she was for ever having her brothers build in the garden, and which constantly fell down about her ears. These evidences of her childish fantasies are entertaining; they suggest the atmosphere in which she grew and her acceptance of it. Her father was a severely holy man, and Avila a place of cloisters and bells, of vespers and funerals, of veil-taking and vow-making; its whole life was characterized by solemn, chivalrous faith and by austere acceptance of the Mysteries of the Church. This child Teresa ran freely in and out of churches where, for instance, the body of Torquemada lay entombed, where the bones of St. Thomas Aquinas were venerated, where the beautiful only son of Queen Isabella was buried – Queen Isabella, conqueror of the Moslem! All recent Christian history must have seemed to the child to lie about her in this little town where the escutcheon of her own family stood for mediaeval faith and glory; it would be odd, I think, if the games and day-dreams of her first innocence did not derive from such an irresistibly dramatic source. Children in Irish Catholic households when I was young played – without a vestige of irreverence – games founded on Mass and Confession and funerals and sermons, as their favourites out of all games, and with not one-tenth of the stimulus to their imaginations that young Teresa de Cepeda had in Avila.

When Doña Beatriz died Teresa, lonely and with her head full of the novels of chivalry which she and her mother had read together – Don Alonso disapproving anxiously of the bad habit – turned the full natural force of her curiosity upon the world and worldly pleasures. She was thirteen, almost marriageable, and very quick and intelligent. There is a tradition that she was a beautiful girl, but the enthusiastic descriptions of her physical characteristics which her contemporaries left behind them do not overmuch persuade a twentieth-century taste; however, that she was spirited, original and wilful is very clear. She rode her mule with a fine seat – how far and hard she was to travel over Spain on mules and donkeys! She played chess as well as any man in Avila; she dressed in vivid colours, and experimented freely with cosmetics. She hid all her mother's novels – *Amadis de Gaul*, *Orlando Furioso* and their fellows (which Cervantes' curate and barber were later on to burn) – from her father's worried eyes, and read and re-read them with passion. (More than that, she tells us that she wrote one.) She became very vain in her dress; snobbish also, about her caste and her 'pure blood';

and she dreamt and thought, and talked, of love.

There were some girl-cousins whose *palacio* almost adjoined her father's. They were very gay, and Teresa loved their company. Don Alonso disapproved of them, but he could not bar them – his brother's children – from his house. With one of these girls, Inez, Ana or Guiomár, Teresa formed a very especial friendship, of which she has much to say in her autobiography.

'...I had a sister much older than myself, from whom, though she was very good and chaste, I learned nothing, whereas from a relative whom we often had in the house I learned every kind of evil.. I became very fond of meeting this woman... she joined me in all my favourite pastimes; and she also introduced me to other pastimes and talked to me about all her conversations and vanities. Until I knew her... I do not think I had ever forsaken God by committing any mortal sin, or lost my fear of God, though I was much more concerned about my honour. This last fear was strong enough to prevent me from forfeiting my honour altogether... nor was there anyone in the world I loved enough to forfeit my honour for... I went to great extremes in my vain anxiety about this, though I took not the slightest trouble about what I must do to live a truly honourable life... the result of my intercourse with this woman was to change me so much that I lost nearly all my soul's natural inclination to virtue, and was greatly influenced by her, and by another person who indulged in the same kinds of pastime... I retained only this concern about my honour, which was a torture to me in everything that I did. When I thought that nobody would ever know, I was rash enough to do many things which were an offence both to my honour and to my God...'

Now, in weighing these and similar passages of Teresa's confessional writings – and she wrote her *Vida* only under the compulsion of obedience to her confessor, and with no idea that she was in fact writing a work which would become a Castilian classic and as familiar to educated Spaniards of the nineteenth and twentieth centuries as, say, *Hamlet* is to Englishmen – it is necessary to exercise caution. Teresa's most learned and careful biographers, from Yepez and Ribera in her own century to Padre Silverio de Santa Teresa in ours, are agreed in reluctance to measure her meaning when she records the sins, if we accept the term, of her adolescence. It must be remembered, first, that the woman writing this autobiography, already in her late forties, was writing it uneasily and only as an imposed penance; but, much more importantly, we must remind ourselves that this woman, when she wrote of her past life, was only then emerging, very anxiously, very wearily and humbly, at the victorious end of a twenty-five years' struggle of the soul; she did not know that she was then already one of the greatest and most honourable among men; she did not know that she had mastered Christian mysticism, she did not know how far and high she had climbed, nor that her perspective on the fourteen-year-old worldling in Avila could only be for ever out of focus for our ordinary eyes. We, reading her ruthless and simple description of the girl she remembers to have been, tend easily to nod our heads and believe we have in a general way, being sinners and experienced, got to the root of her trouble – common enough. But it is not as easy as that. An effort of imagination is required of us here. We have to try to conceive how the curiosities, fantasies and sensual experiments of an averagely worldly adolescence might appear to a woman who had fought a severe, long road to the highest and most exacting form of sanctity and who now, habituated to the beatific vision, believed herself to be, quite simply, the intimate friend of God. It is possible that to one grown so far out of contact with our ordinary human appetites, which once were also hers, those appetites even at their most immature and trivial might seem to her, transfigured before eternity, more shocking, more grotesque and alarming than they could possibly appear to us. It may be in short that Teresa the middle-aged saint overstated her case against Teresa the very young sinner.

Against this argument however we must recall her endowments of detachment and common sense. It is one of the marks of her genius hardest to convey to those who have not read her that this woman, whose flights into the ineffable and incommunicable might even by us, earthbound, be called crazy, never lost hold of her brilliant common sense, nor of her power to stand far back from herself, allowing no facile statement through the net of her self-criticism. It is this exact balance of the scrupulously honest recorder and teacher against the impassioned, tortured mystic that keeps Teresa in her remarkable place in human history. She loved God, believed in Him and was favoured by Him in degrees which we can only accept, with humility, on the evidence of her life and works. But she was a realist and an ironist always; she is never to be caught evading facts or mistaking a hawk for a handsaw; so, if she tells us that in her girlhood she was attached, even inordinately, to the pleasures and adventures of vanity and of the senses, she is probably being as accurate as it was her practice to be, and we need not seek, as some of her pious biographers do, to shield her from her own cool accusations. She is in no need of our defence.

Her father, Don Alonso, did not like her way of life in the years after her mother's death, nor did he care for that girl-cousin from whom, she declares, she was all but inseparable during that phase. Teresa thought that she was cunning in concealing her habits and interests from him, but the pious, anxious man was not as unobservant as she believed him to be.

It was still then the pleasant custom of the Spanish court to make this year one town and next year another its seasonal capital. The Emperor Charles V had not yet discovered that the small, arid village of Madrid suited his health especially well, and he still followed the fashion, set by his grandmother Isabella, of living now in Segovia, now in Toledo, now in Medina del Campo. In the summer of 1531 Charles V was in his German territories, where the monk Martin Luther was causing trouble to church and state; in her husband's absence the Empress Isabel decided that she would try the clear, thin air of Avila for her delicate four-year-old son, Prince Philip – so the court came at the end of May to the high, walled town overlooking the great Mesa. This brilliant event must have been truly exciting for Teresa and her elegant cousins; perhaps it proved somewhat too exciting, because early in July Don Alonso, deciding no doubt that he had had quite enough nonsense from his sixteen-year-old daughter, suddenly marched her out of town and placed her as a boarding scholar in the Augustinian Convent of Our Lady of Grace.

How much it surprised Teresa, this firm action of her father's, we do not know. That at first she was restless, embarrassed and felt herself to be under a cloud we do know. The community lived in extreme austerity, and the young lady scholars committed to their care were very calmly disciplined; there were no novels in this silent house, no cosmetics, and no exciting, confidential friendships.

Teresa looked about her, studied and listened. Soon she observed that she was happy in the house of Our Lady of Grace. 'I was much more content here than in the house of my father.'

*Chapter Three*

# VOCATION

Teresa spent eighteen months as a boarder with the nuns of Our Lady of Grace. The period, as she described it afterwards, looks as if it were quiet, ruminative, indecisive; certainly one feels her changing within it, but changing normally, as any girl might – passing from skittishness and undue preoccupation with self to a more poised and adult phase. She was interested by what she saw in the convent; she admired some of the nuns, and began to question them as to the spring and motive of the religious vocation. She also began to study prayer, its processes and effects – but only with detachment. 'So hard was my heart that if I should read the whole Passion I would not weep a tear. This caused me sorrow.'

She observed the religious life with a sympathy which seems to have surprised her. But she felt no desire whatever to be a nun; 'though', she says, 'I also feared to get married.' The young-romantic phase is over; the realist is beginning to look about her carefully, and to wonder as to the purpose of her life. But after a year and a half of this useful, detached tranquillity, in her eighteenth year she became suddenly, unaccountably ill, and had to return to her father's house from the Convent of Our Lady of Grace.

Youth and normality were over by the end of 1532. She was soon to take her first painful steps towards sanctity, and never to retrace them; and in relation to the immeasurably difficult years which were to make up the rest of her life one sees the eighteen months at Our Lady of Grace as a significant bridge-period, a pause in which much must have been happening to her waiting soul.

It is not possible to diagnose what it was, this first grave illness of Teresa's life. 'A great infirmity' she called it, and left it at that. Perhaps in middle age she who by then had battled with every known and unknown symptom of ill-health could not be bothered to recall the details of her first collapse. Her various afflictions made her very impatient during the extremely active last years of her life. 'This body of mine has never brought me anything but ill.' That was true indeed.

Ill or not, Teresa appears to have been glad enough to return to the world in Avila and to forget her convent school without its walls. But in the spring of 1533 her father took her for convalescence to stay with his brother, Pedro de Cepeda; Uncle Pedro was a fanatically unworldly widower-hermit, who lived in austerity among his mountain shepherds, and whose only reading was the Fathers of the Church. Teresa, who would always rather read anything than nothing, began to study Saint Jerome under Don Pedro's guidance; and together the uncompromising Hermit of Bethlehem and his excessively pious Spanish expositor worked deeply into her spirit. In fact, between them they frightened her. She was weak and ill; we do not know how near she may have gone to death that winter; now in the cold, hushed spring of those uplands of the *paramera* she pondered the sins and frivolities of her short life; more anxiously she pondered the idea of eternity, eternal life, and discussed it with Uncle Pedro. She was a spirit, her faith told her, and could not die. She could not evade the fact of 'for ever'. Life in the human body was brief and troublesome, but it was the endlessness of hereafter, its inescapable endlessness, that had primarily and lastly to be looked to. As a little child Teresa had been frightened by this inexorable 'for ever' and its risks, and had sought martyrdom as the safest means of bargaining with it. Now, a grave and sick young woman, she looked at it longer, and could find no easy way to settle with its terrors. She returned to Avila more ill than when she had left it. She grew very thin; she fainted constantly, constantly she was in fever. She continued to read the Fathers of the Church.

She did not want to be a nun; but she began to understand that she would have to be one. Surprisingly however, when she found enough resolution to tell her father of her intention to join the Carmelite Convent of the Encarnación, he, good, holy man who had been so much troubled by her worldliness, put his foot down and would have none of her idea. It is probable that in a great part of her heart Teresa was relieved by this parental opposition; still, she could not escape from the certainty that she had to be a nun, and after two years of unhappiness, uncertain health and argument with her obdurate father, she ran away from home one morning in 1535, and presented herself as a postulant at the convent gate. And Don Alonso, faced with an accomplished fact, gave in and allowed her to receive the habit of the Mitigated Rule of the Order of Mount Carmel.

Henceforward interest in Teresa, sympathy with her, must be hypothetical. There is no surprise in that. If a man cannot submit himself to the hypothesis 'Let $x=...$' he accepts banishment from mathematics; if he is unable to allow the mystery of the moral law in human beings, he need not plague himself with examination of the tragedies of Shakespeare; if he is assured that the composition of music is dependent on the working of the physical ear, he will not acknowledge the later works of Beethoven. So, if anyone is unable to suspend personal doubt – for that is all it can be – before Teresa's Christian cosmology, such a one will not read of her next twenty-five years except to laugh at her or play psychiatrist.

However, there will be no poet found in such a case, whatever his country, colour, time or creed. She was not a poet, but always, when she strives most scrupulously for precision in recording her raptures, she speaks to poets, anywhere, in any time.

'The kind of vision about which Your Reverence asked me is as follows. She sees nothing either inwardly or outwardly, for the vision is not imaginary. Yet, without seeing anything, the soul understands what it is, and it is pictured to her more clearly than if she were to see it, save that no exact picture is presented to her. It is as if a person were to feel that another is close beside her; and though, because of the darkness, he cannot be seen, she knows for certain that he is there. This, however, is not an exact comparison, for the person who is in the dark knows that the other is there, if not already aware of the fact, either by hearing a sound or by having seen him there previously. But in this case nothing of that kind happens: though not a word can be heard, either exteriorly or interiorly, the soul knows with perfect clearness who is there, where he is, and sometimes what is signified by his presence. Whence he comes and how she cannot tell, but so it is, and for as long as it lasts she cannot cease to be aware of the fact. When the vision leaves her, she cannot recall it to her imagination, however much she may wish to do so; for clearly if she could it would be a case of imagination and not of actual presence, to recapture which is not in her power; and so it is with all supernatural matters...

'On one occasion, when I was reciting the Hours with the Community, my soul suddenly became recollected and seemed to me to become bright all over like a mirror: no part of it – back, sides, top or bottom – but was completely bright, and in the centre of it was a picture of Christ Our Lord as I generally see Him. I seemed to see Him in every part of my soul as clearly as in a mirror, and this mirror – I cannot explain how – was wholly sculptured in the same Lord by a most loving communication which I shall never be able to describe...

'Once when I was in prayer I saw, for a very brief time and without any distinctness of form, but with perfect clarity, how all things are seen in God and how within Himself He contains them all. Describe this I cannot... I cannot say with certainty that I saw nothing, for, as I am able to make this comparison, something must have been visible to me; but the vision comes in so subtle and delicate a way that the understanding cannot grasp it... Let me say that the Godhead is like a very clear diamond, much larger than the whole world, or a mirror, like that which symbolized the soul in my account of an earlier vision, except that it is of a far sublimer kind, to which I cannot do justice. Let us suppose, furthermore, that all we do is seen in this diamond, which is of such a kind that it contains everything within itself, because there is nothing capable of falling outside such greatness. It was a terrifying experience for me, in so short a space of time, to see so many things at once in the clear depths of that diamond.'

Teresa, the young, uneasy nun beginning a life which was, despite her obstinate will to embrace it, repugnant to her senses and her lively tastes, was lucky in that her imagination was naturally rooted in Christian doctrine. The Trinity, Father, Son and Holy Ghost, and all the saints and angels stemming out from all that the Trinity implies, were to Teresa from her cradle to her grave as indispensably natural as her own breath – and as little to be questioned or explained as we would say are the daisies in the grass. God and the Saints were her hypothesis; indeed, they were her axiom. But, since we have mentioned daisies, it is pleasing to recall that once she said, when endeavouring to explain the practice of the Prayer of Quiet, that she was helped thereto if she could 'look at a field, or flowers, or water'.

She, who was most complicated and of whom fierce trials were to be exacted, was lucky in the brilliance of her faith. She was lucky too in that she could with such grace, modesty and precision record its workings in her soul. But 'luck' is not a fair word to use about Teresa. Whatever she won from her vision of life, whatever she left us, she bought at a price. Like her colleague, John of the Cross, she asked for suffering, and her prayer was answered.

No ordinary person, no creature of the world, can other than most anxiously attempt even to outline to other ordinary persons the known facts of Teresa's life between 1535 and 1560. From the latter year until her death in 1582 she was a public figure, a fighter, a politician, a contender with the visible forces of her time, a soldier, wit and controversialist whose fame spread rapidly over Europe. Such a character, were it not for the accident, let us say, of its pure sanctity, should be comparatively easy to rough-sketch in a personal portrait. But as in the sanctity is the catch, so in the long period wherein sanctity was assaulted, or, more exactly, wherein sanctity made assault on her half-reluctant soul, we must look for most of the pros and cons of her peculiar greatness. It is an alarming territory, very difficult to survey.

During her first year as a religious Teresa's health forsook her inexplicably. She does not appear to have been spiritually unhappy, or other than secure in her decision to be a nun – yet her heart, her nerves, her digestion and her muscular system all began in this year to be racked and reduced by pains and symptoms very difficult to explain. Attacks of catalepsy and prolonged periods of near-catalepsy baffled all the doctors of Avila, and her father obtained permission to take her to the mountains again, there to undergo treatment by a famous *curandera*, or woman-quack.

It was during this year, which she spent in semi-seclusion, preparing for and undergoing her terrible 'cure', that she began to examine the processes of prayer, and through much reading to find her way to meditation and to the Prayer of Recollection. But in this year she also had one serious struggle with those desires of the senses and thoughts of earthly love which had occupied her, normally and strongly, in girlhood.

The parish priest in her mountain retreat was a man of intelligence and of some learning. 'I have always been attracted by learning... After I had begun to make my confessions to this priest... he took an extreme liking to me.' Friendship grew between them. The priest was, had been for years, the lover of a woman in the neighbourhood. 'The fact that he had lost his honour and his good name was quite well known... I was sorry for him because I liked him very much.'

The two fought through a dangerous situation, in which clearly each felt attraction and affection for the other, and wherein they acted with frankness and good sense. Teresa was safe enough, no doubt; she had chosen God and the Carmelite rule with her eyes wide open; yet sudden friendship, which finally she used to bring her confessor back to his vows and his priestly obligations, had danger in it at which she did not blink.

The 'cure' all but killed her. 'At the end of two months, the severity of the remedies had almost ended my life.' Her bewildered father hurried her back to Avila and the professional doctors, who declared that now, as well as all her other nameless ailments, she had a consumption. Tortured, reduced to skin and bone, drifting without intermission between ague and high fever, doubled almost in two with muscular pain, at last one day she passed into a catalepsy so absolute and prolonged that the lookers-on were left with nothing more to do than prepare her obsequies and dig her grave.

But after four days she opened her eyes and spoke, and thereafter through a terrible, agonized period of death-in-life fought back to life and to her real preparation for what it was to ask of her. (In her account of this extraordinary illness her dry humour does not desert her. When she says: 'My only alleviation was that if no one came near me my pains often ceased' we glimpse what sixteenth-century nursing may sometimes have seemed like to the nursed.)

Eight months after her return to Avila in a dying state she re-entered the Convent of the Encarnación. She was almost totally paralysed, but able to pray and think, and she rejoiced in restoration to conventual life. Very gradually the paralysis left her; within a year she could move about on her hands and knees. 'My great yearning, I think, was to get well so that I might be alone when I prayed – there was no possibility of this in the infirmary.' It was three years before she was able to live as a normally active member of the community, and for the remainder of her days her body in its weakness was to devise and plot unremittingly but without success against the winged energies of her strong soul. Ill-health, in several forms, must henceforward be taken for granted in her lifestory; for Teresa gives us almost as little time to pause and note it as she allowed herself.

In her first active years at the Encarnación, her paralysis gone and comparative health restored, the sociable, quick-witted creature took community life with zest, finding that it truly stimulated her; and, according to her anxious, later account, she took the Mitigated Rule of her Order as she found it, and thought that normal observance of it might suffice for peace of mind, and for salvation. But it is always necessary to take Teresa's views on herself with caution. She was a natural perfectionist, unaware that her standard in any undertaking was extremely high. She thought – according to her autobiography – that for many years she was a normally good, variable, middle-of-the-way religious; but I believe that no honest, experienced religious would agree with her, on the evidence.

She watched herself always; she was self-conscious in a merciless fashion never attempted by the average person.

'This belief which they had that I was not so wicked was the result of them seeing me, young though I was... withdrawing myself frequently into solitude, saying my prayers... which gave me the appearance of being virtuous. I myself was vain and liked to be thought well of in the things wont to be esteemed by the world... I think it was a very bad thing for me not to be in a convent that was enclosed ... for when a convent follows standards and allows recreations which belong to the world, and the obligations of the nuns are so ill understood, the Lord has perforce to call each of them individually, and not once but many times, if they are to be saved...

'I was once in the company of a certain person, right at the beginning of my acquaintance with her, when the Lord was pleased to make me realize that these friendships were not good for me, and to warn me and enlighten my great blindness. Christ revealed himself to me in an attitude of great sternness, and showed me what there was in this that displeased Him. I saw Him with the eyes of the soul more clearly than I could ever have seen Him with those of the body; and it made such an impression upon me that, although it is now more than twenty-six years ago, I seem to have Him present with me still. I was greatly astonished and upset about it, and I never wanted to see that person again... However, just because the vision did not please me, I forced myself to give the lie to my own instinct and... as great importunity was brought to bear on me I entered into relations with that person once again... In subsequent occasions I got to know other people in the same way; I spent many years in this pestilential pastime, which, whenever I was engaged in it, never seemed to me as bad as it really was, though sometimes I saw clearly that it was not good. But no one caused me as much distraction as did the person of whom I am speaking, for I was very fond of her.'

The Convent of the Encarnación was large, rich and over-inhabited by daughters of the aristocratic houses of Castile. Perhaps its rule was not lax, as laxity was measured in religious houses of its period; but it *was* easy, and its *locutorios* and gardens were constantly loud and gay with the voices and gossiping of abbots, friars, and great ladies. Teresa was all her life sociable, and enjoyed the enjoyment which she could cause in others; it is impossible to read her letters without being made aware of her social gifts, her sense of comedy, her fluent irony, and her warmth of heart. Moreover – she is insistent upon this – she was vain, desired persistently to be liked, desired to please. And here in this Carmelite house she re-discovered that which she had earlier found out as a boarder at Our Lady of Grace, that conventual life with women suited her well, was indeed far more to her taste than the normal kind of social life she had attacked so zestfully in her father's house. Yet she was also imperatively attracted to the life of prayer, and to the contemplative rule by which she had in perfect honesty undertaken to live. She could not escape, she never was to escape from her pure desire of God.

'On the one hand, God was calling me. On the other, I was following the world. All the things of God gave me great pleasure, yet I was tied and bound to those of the world. It seemed as if I wanted to reconcile these two contradictory things, so completely opposed to one another – the life of the spirit and the pleasures and joys and pastimes of the senses. I suffered great trials in prayer, for the spirit was not master in me, but slave. I could not, therefore, shut myself up within myself (the procedure in which consisted my whole method of prayer) without at the same time shutting in a thousand vanities. I spent many years in this way, and now I am amazed that a person could have gone on for so long without giving up either the one or the other. I know quite well that by that time it was no longer in my power to give up prayer, because He who desired me for His own in order to show me greater favours held me Himself in His hand.'

It was indeed a long battle, so long and so hard on her that the forces engaged must have been well matched. Now Teresa was always, whatever her other impulses, most poetically and irresistibly attracted to her own vision of God, and to the difficult idea of living in His love and His presence, therefore those parts in her which, within the conventual rule, withheld her in fluctuating struggle over more than twenty years from her full vocation cannot have been slight or ordinary. A disposition to sociability would not have been enough to hold the ardent and forthright creature back in twenty years from full acceptance of her own ideal; and it is clear that weaknesses so passive as indolence or a wish to conform to whatever was average among nuns could not have counted at all against her spiritual certainty and hunger. No; we have said that her genius was for life – and if that is true then all the elements which *are* life were well mixed in her; and that is why her struggle towards perfection was as fierce and prolonged as her conquest of it was complete. She is not explicit in her writings about the particular 'pastimes of the senses' to which she confesses her long addiction, but we may take her cool word for it that she knew as well what she talked of in their regard as she did in other contexts; she was never a scarlet sinner, a Mary Magdalen (a saint who attracted her strong sympathy); and although she read *The Confessions of Saint Augustine* with marked understanding and appreciation – 'I seemed to see myself in them' – we can be certain that she, a most carefully brought-up Spanish lady of the sixteenth century, could never have had any such acquaintance with sensual pleasures as the Bishop of Hippo allowed himself in his youth. But assuredly it was love, human love and her idea of it, which was the chief enemy between her and her love of God. Probably, like Saint Augustine, Teresa was, at her most tempted, always more in love with love than with any fellow creature; she suggests of herself that she was moody and restless in attachments. Yet she formed many of them, and chiefly with women, whose devotion, as her active years were to prove, she could always and effortlessly command. These friendships which in her youth delighted and in her young womanhood as a professed nun so much troubled and impeded her, prepared her in great measure no doubt for that part of her life which from her cell in the Encarnación was not to be foreseen. In order to become a saint she had to overcome and forgo them; but in order to become the Reformer of the Order of Our Lady of Carmel, it was perhaps necessary for her to have known them, and through them all that of herself and of human nature which they revealed to her.

'If only I could describe the occasions of sin during these years from which God delivered me... and how He continually saved me from the danger of losing my entire reputation!... This happened because He Who knows all things saw it to be necessary, in order that hereafter I might be given some credence when speaking of things that concern His service. This sovereign bounty regarded not my great sins but the desires I had to serve Him and my grief at not having in myself the strength to turn the desires into actions.'

It is not easy to map the course of Teresa's life between 1543 and 1561. In the former year her father died, and also during it she overcame the inexplicable paralysis which had cut her off from the normal life of her sisters in religion; and in the latter she founded the first house of her Reform, became a rebel and a portent of the Counter-Reformation. In the period between these dates her spirit, or rather her personality, must be considered at first as moving along two divided planes, and in its later years rapt up into the higher one, the region of pure mysticism to which her mastery of the Prayer of Union carried her, out of reach of that normal self which she was not to unlearn there or forget, and whose hard lessons she was indeed to take forward with her, as a great part of her ammunition, into twenty years of earthly trouble.

She believed, from the first thought of her life to the last, in the Christian God and in the whole cosmology of Christian doctrine. But her accurate development and expression through herself of what that belief was is analogous to an artist's self-conscious exploitation of his gift. It is in fact in her the scrupulous and inescapable exploitation of a gift. Many people can paint, more or less well; many can compose a tune or a song; many can write a novel or a love-poem; and many, many people believe in God and pray to Him. But Rembrandt, Beethoven, Shakespeare and Dostoevsky are lonely, isolated geniuses, and so are Teresa of Avila and her friend John of the Cross. The achievements of those men who have overtopped mankind will always, and rightly, receive mankind's lip-service, at least; but when they have used the stuff we know, and spun their marvels proudly from themselves – and we know them, after all, to be made of our clay – we can, or anyhow we do, venture on quite bold appraisals of them. But to advance into the very face and presence of God, and to insist that it is He who invites the audacity; to talk and walk with Him, and truthfully and coolly memorize such intimacy in all its phases, and coolly write it down – this is mysticism, this is a territory that millions would choose never to glimpse, let alone examine; and it is understandable if some find even Teresa's unflurried chartings of it alarming. It is not everyone's land, however radiantly it gleam. Just as for many of us there can never be other than darkness and horror in the major expressions of Indian Buddhism, or as for others no imaginable translation will ever convey the essence of a Chinese lyric; or, to come nearer home, as some will not be brought to read the great, exploratory work of Marcel Proust, or to look with any hope or any patience at the later canvases of Picasso, so what Teresa found in the world of prayer which she so carefully cultivated, what she found, made and left behind for her fellow men, does not by any means appeal to all her fellow men. And no one would be less surprised at this than Teresa. She was for ever, in her later life, warning against the false assaults of the pious upon mystical experience.

'But when I hear servants of God, men of weight, learning and intelligence, making a fuss because God is not giving them devotion, it revolts me to listen to them. I do not mean that, when God gives them such a thing, they ought not to accept it and set a great store by it, because in that case His Majesty must know that it is good for them. But I do mean that if they do not receive it they should not be distressed; they should realize that, as His Majesty does not give it them, it is unnecessary; they should be masters of themselves and go on their way.'

Teresa entered her mystic period through no accident, but because she was intellectually attracted to the exercise of prayer, and because her will decided that she explore and study the fruitful, exacting experiences she encountered in such exercise. So while still at first living the outward life of the crowded, worldly Encarnación, and battling emotionally, as we have seen, with her own pleasure in its laxities, her mind, always formidably honest, was rigorously, secretly engaged in the experiment of prayer.

She has written with incomparable lucidity of this science of the spirit, beginning with her own beginnings in it, until, in the sum of her mystical works and on their shining peaks, we recognize that all has been said of communication with God that can be said in words. One supposes that every educated Christian has at some time been instructed on prayer through the medium of her famous image of a garden and the ways of watering it. This is a very simple piece of writing.

'It seems to me that the garden can be watered in four ways: by taking the water from a well, which costs us great labour; or by a waterwheel and buckets, when the water is drawn by a windlass... or by a stream or a brook, which waters the ground much better, for it saturates it more thoroughly... or by heavy rain, when the Lord waters it with no labour of ours.'

A child can reflect on the four progressive movements of this parallel, but a poet, advanced and impetuous in imagination, will also see how far into the movements of the soul its clear ascent might carry him.

The Teresa of whom I am seeking to give my personal portrait is the completed Teresa, the great one, the accomplished saint and soldier, the Teresa of 1563 and onwards – the Teresa of San José in Avila who, having made herself into master of all trades, was henceforth content also to be the jack of many of them as occasion required, and who sought for the remaining nineteen years of her life to live outwardly, as no other mystic could, so as to bring to her fellow men that which she herself had found and now saw to be the sole good – the vision of God. But before we find that fully-grown and extremely lively saint, we have to consider the earlier, the tormented and alarming one, out of whom she grew. Not so as to understand her. That is not possible. Teresa, most brilliantly comprehensible to us sometimes, most deceptively vivid, or touching, or forthright, or silly, is in her sum not to be humanly understood. But she can be known – that is to say, we are in possession of a large body of facts about her, and, these considered, we can then either accept her as an amazing example of human possibilities, or reject her as irrelevant, or disconcerting, or as a deranged invalid. But – for a deranged invalid – she succeeded so unusually (*a*) as a writer and (*b*) as a religious reformer, that it is unlikely that the intelligently curious will stick to those epithets.

They were applied to her, however, again and again while she lived; and often by wise and holy men who understood her talent for sanctity, but who dared not accept some of its extreme and perilous forms of expression – any more than she dared accept them herself. Not without superficial cause, this general fear of her experiences – least of all is her own fear of them to be wondered at. She had friends indeed, within the convent and without; but as she inexorably advanced into those phases and explorations of prayer which afterwards she was to describe so lucidly, she must too often have seemed to herself and others simply a lunatic. So did Gandhi often seem, within our recent memories, to us of the west who learnt before his death to call him saint. So can John Wesley still seem, to even the most admiring readers of his Journal; so does George Fox bewilder us even now.

Teresa bewildered her contemporaries. In twenty years she became increasingly to all around her – except a few anxious friends – a wonder, an irritation, a scandal and a menace. She saw herself that this mounting state of affairs was true, and natural; and in prayer and in the counsel of her confessors she battled to escape from herself – whatever that term might mean.

She had visions from the beginning; rather, she was invaded by conditions of awareness of God which she defines and redefines in her writings – attempting to separate 'imaginary' experiences, which she doubts and deplores, from 'intellectual', which she accepts as irresistible, coming as they do from outside unprompted by any echo of emotion. These visions developed; she conversed with the Trinity, she was, to her horror, lifted off the ground in prayer, she endured trance, translation and transfixion; she saw hell – more particularized, more brief and small her reports of hell than what Dante saw, yet it is evident that nothing that he told of the *malebolge* would have surprised her. But neither could Wordsworth have told her anything that she had not already reported, in her modest prose, of the suspension of the senses, and the flight of the spirit out of their reach into ecstasy. Again and again, anxiously, she begs us to understand this experience, when sense is arrested and the soul takes charge. She writes more simply and more often than Wordsworth does of the faculties being laid asleep, and of some other, diviner system being imposed upon human consciousness. Her attempts to record in plain prose the serenity of some of these moments of acceptance are, I think, superb, at once because of their modesty and their strange success:

'It is not a radiance which dazzles, but a soft whiteness and an infused radiance which, without wearying the eyes, causes them the greatest delight; nor are they wearied by the brightness which they see in seeing this divine beauty. So different from any earthly light is the brightness and light now revealed to us that... the brightness of our sun seems quite dim... Not that the sun or any other such light enters into the vision: on the contrary, it is like a natural light and all other kinds of light seem artificial. It is a light which never gives place to night, and, being always light, is disturbed by nothing.'

Within this light, which Rilke would have recognized, she sets for us her innocent and amazing interviews with God. Interviews in which 'His Majesty', as she called Christ, sometimes spoke with a bluntness very like her own: as, for instance, when she complained to Him of some one of her characteristic faults – 'Daughter, there is no help for that.' Someone to whom lately I was quoting some of His Majesty's remarkable snubs to Teresa observed – 'A vivid projection of her own personality!'

Written down by the elderly, triumphant nun who as she wrote saw the *purpose* of her mystical life and what she had to make of it – the story of the struggling years is a bright flowering track across our normal arid life. But while being undergone, while being witnessed, these years were trouble and woe; terror, scandal, gossip and hysteria.

So it is always; so it will always be, one way or another, with genius. Sappho did not run to common form; neither did Catherine of Siena; neither did Emily Brontë nor Emily Dickinson. And neither of course – but that causes less annoyance – did any *man* of genius, ever.

The Convent of the Encarnación was overcrowded, and the private life of the true contemplative was neither possible in it nor was it encouraged. While Teresa struggled in embarrassment and fear to conceal and subdue the outward strange signs of her especial condition, as she went from confessor to confessor, and tried first this new discipline, then that or the other form of, or abstention from, prayer – she was, naturally, observed. Other nuns, no doubt disliking from the first her apparent pretensions to great sanctity, grew to resent and fear its embarrassing signs. The parlours of the house, and soon the town, and in the end all of Castile and the royal court itself hummed with stories of the *beata* of Avila.

The *beata* herself was not surprised at this; and in spite of frequent visitations to her spirit which by their irresistible serenity persuaded over and over again that it was God who sought her, and not the powers of evil, she was often unable to adhere to this certainty; she was sometimes immeasurably depressed, exhausted and ashamed, as well as ill. The various holy men who struggled to understand her were for the most part as much puzzled by her as she was herself; and they were also quite practically alarmed.

The Holy Office of the Inquisition, which ruled Spain mercilessly for Queen Isabella at the close of the fifteenth century, had lapsed into comparative indolence in the early years of the sixteenth, until in the 1540's a great scandal arose about a nun in Córdoba. This woman, having hoaxed many theologians as to her sanctity, having become a cult of the royal family, and bearing on her body wounds resembling the stigmata of St. Francis of Assisi, had finally been brought before the Holy Office and made sensational confessions – as to devil worship, illusionism and curious sexual practices – which, richly embroidered were borne all over Spain, and created a scandal which lasted, enjoyably, a very long time. Naturally too it started up a hue and cry after *alumbradas, beatas* and their kind; and the Holy Office was made busy again as zealots reported their suspicions and their finds. So that it behoved anyone more saintly than his neighbour to look carefully to his outward expressions of sanctity, and keep them pitched to what the man in the street allowed.

Teresa, to her embarrassment, was not able to do this. 'His Majesty began to grant me frequently the Prayer of Quiet and often too the Prayer of Union, which lasted for a long time. As there have been cases recently in which women have been subjected by the devil to serious illusions and deceptions, I began to be afraid, for the delight and the sweetness which I felt were so great and often I could not help feeling them. But I was conscious of a very deep inward assurance that this was of God.'

Teresa was not afraid of the Inquisition. Indeed, when her first writings, her *Vida* and *Camino de Perfección*, appeared and some theologian told her that he feared the Holy Office might send for her now, she was very much interested, and said that if he thought there was anything in her work which was wrong or needed elucidation she would like to go at once and present herself before the Grand Inquisitor, that she was entirely at that prelate's disposition. It has been said that it was the report of this cool and friendly wish to convenience the Holy Office instantly – very surprising to the anxious theologian – which, in part at least, decided the Council of the Inquisition against examining her. Certainly all who knew her seem, from their records and comments, to have known that the troublesome woman was not afraid of earthly threats or dangers. But she *was* afraid of misleading herself; she *was* afraid of presuming that neurotic and unmanageable experiences of mind and body were from God.

Avila, however – the aristocratic nuns of the Encarnación and their ambitious and orthodox friends and relations – Avila was, like any normal social unit, afraid of a scandal, much afraid of being held up to mockery and danger in Castile. The Lutheran panic was up in Spain in the 1550's; certain *alumbrados* had been found to hold Luther's dogma on good works. While Prince Philip was still absent in the Netherlands and old Charles V was over-eating, playing with clocks and making his soul in the monastery of Yuste, the Regent Princess Juana was an enthusiastic promoter of *autos da Fé* and heresy hunts.

Now while doubtless some exasperated Avilans thought that to play a leading role in an *auto da Fé* would merely be the price of Teresa de Ahumada and what she had been asking for only too long, it is also doubtless that she not only had some faithful friends, but that she could without effort disarm enemies. Her sincerity, her modesty and her humour became as crystal-clear in any one conversation as did her uncanny intelligence. (For proof of this one has only to look in any of the writings of her contemporaries about her – or better still in her own letters.) Moreover, Avila did not want a scandal.

So, clerics were sent for from far and wide, to examine her, to discipline, to consult, to hear her confessions. Some of them were wise men, some were foolish; she submitted herself under obedience to them all. All were rigorous with her; none could confound her curious, easy power in theological argument; she seems to have been – as it were by accident – the most orthodox of Catholics. The whole labour of the Council of Trent would have been as nothing to her; she knew her way all round and through the intricate religion of which she was a member. They had no Lutheran here, no *alumbrada*; yet her states of prayer continued, and she continued to say, without explanation, such things as this: 'Once, when I was reciting the Psalm *Quicunque vult* I was shown so clearly how it was possible for there to be one God alone and Three Persons that it caused me both amazement and much comfort.'

She was forbidden to read certain theological works. Her books were taken from her, and their loss caused her great distress. Alternatively, under another confessor, she was allowed suddenly far more freedom than even the most wilful members of her community assumed, and actually in the last three years of her life at Encarnación, she was permitted to live, as a nun and following her own severe rule, in the house of her faithful friend Doña Guiomár de Ulloa, a rich widow of Avila, who was later to serve her Reform with passionate loyalty and generosity.

It is probable that this curious permission to a nun of an enclosed Order was prompted partly by the advice of some confessor who felt Teresa's very great need to be alone and to pray alone, and partly by the willingness of exasperated and lazy superiors to have the 'ecstatic' out of the way as much as possible.

Some of her spiritual directors were severely afflicting to her. Of one good Jesuit she said good-humouredly: 'I love this Father of mine, but he has a bad disposition.' Another, whose name she never revealed, made a real fool of himself. He could not bear her accounts of vision, or of the Prayer of Union, and was convinced her experiences were, through no fault of hers, from the devil. It is truly hard to follow what this fussy man had in mind, but he commanded his penitent at every intimation of a supernatural presence 'to give him the fig'. Now, 'to give the fig, is an old, well-known gesture of obscenity; it is a Spanish insult – 'Fig me like the bragging Spaniard', says Pistol – and Teresa must have known in some measure, however correct a Spanish lady she was, that it was a dreadful gesture. The hideous absurdity of the poor confessor's idea embarrasses us, even at this long distance. However, obedience or no obedience, Teresa could not make the gesture. Instead, she lifted up her crucifix and said aloud: 'Come on! I am God's servant; let me see what you can do to me!'

From about that time – 1560 – she seems to have shaken off the power of officially appointed confessors. She says that at last about this time she became certain that she was chosen to work for 'His Majesty'. Her fears, her devils left her – not for ever, but never again to darken, even momentarily, her certainty of God's especial friendship. 'I have acquired an authority over them, bestowed upon me by the Lord of all, so that they are no more trouble to me now than flies.'

Light – not the great light of heaven within which she had long been wont to pray – but light such as we all seek wherein to decide our actions, invested Teresa now, and brought her to self-reliance. She advanced, in spirit though not yet in plan, into a new era, her great, her last twenty years. But she did not say goodbye to the woeful period of doubts and devils without a free-and-easy slap at some of the wellmeaning directors of those days.

'Whatever are we thinking of? I am quite sure I am more afraid of people who are themselves terrified of the devil than I am of the devil himself. For he cannot harm me in the least, whereas they, *especially if they are confessors*, can upset people a great deal, and for several years they were such a trial to me that I marvel now that I was able to bear it. Blessed be the Lord...'

*Chapter Four*

## 'MARTHA AND MARY WALKING ABOUT TOGETHER'

We have reached, as longwindedly as sketchily, the point we were making for, when all the faculties of one strange nature suddenly knit themselves into a purpose, and become life greatly manifested.

In a conversation with two or three young nuns, or aspirants to the veil, a conversation like many others, in the house of her friend Guiomár de Ulloa, Teresa announced her decision to reform the Carmelite Order. But not before the youngest girl present had said that that could be done.

Let us look back. The original rule of the Carmelites, though set down and known, had long been lost to the Order. The story of its foundation, in the twelfth century, by a group of hermits at the foot of Mount Carmel is rich in legends of the prophet Elias, who is said to have directed an Italian monk to found a place of hermitage on the site of his former dwelling. The first hermits believed themselves protected and directed in all things by the prophet; and they had a rule of life drawn up for them in the early thirteenth century by Albert, Patriarch of Jerusalem. This was later to be known as the Primitive Rule of the Order of Mount Carmel. Among its sixteen articles, chief were these: a ban on property, a ban on meat; a command that each hermit live in a cell by himself, and that all live by manual labour, and in silence. Further a strict fast was to be kept, except on Sundays, from 14th September of each year until Easter Day of the next.

The growth of the Mohammedan power in Palestine in the thirteenth century made peaceful life difficult for Christian hermits, and so the Carmelites abandoned Carmel and faced westward. They established themselves and their rule in Cyprus, in France, in England. I believe that their first English foundation was in Kent, in 1245. Certainly at that period an Englishman, St. Simon Stock, was a very successful General of the Order.

In Europe it was found necessary for the members of each group to live communally rather than in separated hermitages. This meant abandonment of the rule of total silence, and was the first mitigation. Also, they became in the thirteenth century a mendicant order, and, by reason of the white cloak and scapular which they wore over their brown habit, they were known as the White Friars.

They grew powerful throughout Europe, especially in England when, under various Papal mitigations, they acquired wealth and lands. At the time of the dissolution of the monasteries, the Carmelites possessed fifty-two English houses. There were many internal schisms and disputes as the Order grew, but on the whole the tendency towards mitigation, and laxity, kept the lead. Early in the fifteenth century communities of Carmelite nuns were founded, and these markedly upheld the already strong tendency towards mitigation, and continued in mitigating what was now officially known as the Mitigated Rule of Mount Carmel. By the close of the fifteenth century this powerful mendicant order of White Friars (and nuns) had travelled far indeed from the silent hermitages of Palestine and the admonitions of the prophet.

And then came the sixteenth century, bringing with it the Reformation, the Renaissance, the Council of Trent; and Martin Luther and Teresa of Avila.

When Luther died in 1546 Teresa was in her thirty-second year, and no more than a sick, unhappy tormented, unimportant nun. But she regarded him as the arch-enemy of civilization, and it can hardly be doubted that when the news of his death reached the Encarnación Convent she rejoiced exceedingly, and thanked 'His Majesty' with all her burning heart. She amuses us, in her writings, with her careless use of the word 'Lutherans'. She simply flings it out, without a thought of accuracy, at any supposed enemy of the Church. As we now, with sifted, loaded justification, centuries old, say 'Vandals' or 'Philistines', she, with no vestige of such excuse, simply said 'Lutherans'. This sweeping carelessness was part of a pose she had. She, who could be, they all testified, accurate and sure-footed as an attacking puma, or, if you like, as a leading counsel for defence, when under fire from Inquisitor or Papal Nuncio, or Provincial of the Mitigated Order, liked sometimes to sweep precision all aside and say what happened to suit her. Whoever was against her was a 'Lutheran', just as we, according to our time or place, may call out 'Sassenach' or 'Hun' or 'Red'. This is amusing, at our distance from her inaccuracy; nevertheless I for one do not excuse it in a woman of genius. Any more than I excuse her lapses into the 'I am only a woman and therefore...' line of argument. That way round, which she often used in letters to spiritual directors and other men, may simply have been guile; but Teresa, however Castilian and man-ridden was her upbringing, *must* have observed as she grew that by reason of what she was, she could make her father, her brothers, her confessors and all her male confronters do as she wished. I have never excused in her these low bows of the 'poor little woman'. When she slaps down her more or less intelligent nuns I am also out of sympathy with her; though then I see her dictatorial and subtle point. She was directing a peculiarly difficult campaign, and in its essentials it was restorative, conservative; its intention was back to modesty, back to silence, back to death of the self; back to the presence of God. That being understood, granted her own free, arrogant and slapdash use of all her intellectual powers, she was entitled on her terms of reference to ask surrender of individual thought from her followers – *not*, let it be said, and she *never* asked it – surrender of the self to *her* instruction, but only surrender to what they had come seeking, the voice and presence of God. Certainly she asked no one for obedience to her, or to any law their own souls had not led them towards. But she was somewhat too arrogant to those who, in their human frailty (so like her own) showed a disposition to think. 'God forbid that any of my daughters should be *latinas*,' she said, as we nowadays should say 'bluestockings', or 'intellectuals'. And, to a young woman who sought to join one of her foundations and who asked if she might bring with her her own copy of the Old Testament, which she was studying, she said: 'No, my child. Don't come to us with your Bible.' And rightly, as we think from where we sit now, the young woman withdrew politely with her Bible, and sought no more to join the Reformed Carmelites.

All of this is not a vague digression. It arises from and leads me back to Teresa's loathing of Luther – of whom, let it be said, she knew no more than could any ordinary person in Avila in the 1530's and 1540's. And if the point I desire to make causes that great saint to turn once again in her grave, no one could be more apologetic than I. Those bones, so weary when they went to rest, have been sufficiently tormented by the devout; yet I risk suggesting that the great reformer Teresa had gifts and attributes in common with her enemy, Martin Luther. She was a Castilian lady, and therefore had beautiful manners, which he sadly lacked; she also had a subtle kind of humour, which was not his, and she was fine when he was coarse. But she was, like Luther, passionate, fearless and self-assured; like him she was a naturally brilliant and fluent writer, who did not have to struggle with the art of writing, and who wrote only to forward immediate business; like Luther too she was the master of her fellows, and perhaps more consciously than he, certainly with more guile, she was, when it suited her, a dictator. And it would no doubt horrify her to hear that in her utter singleness of purpose, in her sheer passion to serve God, she resembled Luther.

But Luther was fifteen years dead when she finally, decisively spoke up, and ranged herself, on her own terms, in his place.

I am not seeking here to be paradoxical or to give offence. When Luther went to work his intention was precisely what Teresa's was to be later. His temperament and his career, creating between them a certain set of accidents, carried him far from his first moorings, but in his early movements of reform he was all faith, all passionate devotion to Mother Church. Teresa had the advantage of him – in breeding, let us venture to say; certainly in social training. Also she was a woman and conservative; also, her impulse for reform was backward to the old, forgotten austerities – not forward to their overthrow and dismissal. Nevertheless as she sweeps along to her final work, praying, impatiently yet warmly, for all 'Lutherans' and such, overriding all material scruples, laughing at caution, hurting others as she was ready to hurt herself, asking and giving the impossible, and fantastically sure at last in her forty-ninth year of 'His Majesty's' Will, we cannot but be reminded of the attributes which her enemy had brought to *his* reform. And when she founded her first convent of the Primitive Rule – that little house of San José in Avila – with her four or five young followers, when by this simple, necessary gesture she threw Avila, the Carmelite Order and the Spanish hierarchy into a confusion that was to be fierce and long drawn out – she could have said in perfect truth, with Luther: *'Hier stehe ich; ich kann nicht anders.'*

It is pleasant to know that the first five years of her great reforming period were happy years. In 1562 she founded her little convent of San José in Avila. Into it she received five young novices, and began her reform. How and why she was allowed, by the Bishop of Avila, by the Prioress of El Encarnación or by the Provincial of the Carmelite Order, to make this revolutionary gesture is not explicable, at this distance. We have seen that she was already allowed exceptional freedom of action – for herself; we have seen that she was to orthodox Avila a problem and an anxiety. That her Bishop and the authorities of her Order allowed her to accept from friends the little humble house in north Avila and there to attempt, subject always to the general Carmelite authority, the enforcement of the ancient, severe rule on four or five young zealots, proves no more than that she was a problem, that someone of good sense, probably the Bishop of Avila, thought that at least no harm could come of her attempt, and that in any case this remarkable, alarming nun would never be contained in the lax cloister of El Encarnación. And no doubt at El Encarnación the vote was to let her go, and make such a fool of herself as she might choose.

So she went off across the town, to total poverty, irresponsibility, faith in 'His Majesty', faith in her few friends – also, she went off to her own great, pure intention, to her saintly destiny, and, for a start, to five happy years. She has told us that the years at San José, before the wide responsibilities of her gesture assaulted her, were the happiest she ever knew. And everything she records of them affirms that. This is understandable. After a long period of tormented anxiety she had made a difficult, but simple, decision. That decision made seemed then conclusive and sufficient. Its consequences, in earthly conflict, were for a while concealed. Peacefully, as she prayed and sang and scrubbed floors with her five young nuns, she imagined that the personal gesture was enough, that God was content that she and her few friends were living as nearly as they could the ideal life of Carmel, that that was what was required of her, and that in finding this way to live she had answered the fierce exactions of the years in which 'His Majesty' had tortured her.

Let not the phrases 'happy years' and 'the happiest she knew' mislead us here. Nor should the picture of her praying, singing and scrubbing floors be taken to *cover* the first five years of her attempt at Carmelite reform. All human statements about happiness are relative and subjective; and Teresa was not in pursuit of it, as we know – but did accidentally enjoy its gleams in these especial years, and accepted them gratefully. And, with health somewhat restored, with a practical purpose in view, with battle in the bright Castilian air, and with the dawning discovery that she could write, as she sat down under obedience to try to explain herself to her confessor – it is probable that she felt her hitherto scattered and bewildering forces coming together with design.

The five years were broken; she was not allowed to be always with her neophytes at San José; she was subject to the general Carmelite rule; she was sent hither and thither, and had to confront this cleric and that, one prelate and another. She was under observation, under question, and standing in the light, the often merciless light of contemporary Castile.

But she had San José; she had an idea ever widening into purpose; she had the counsel of one of the purest of all ascetics, Peter Alcántara, Franciscan reformer and saint; she had the obligatory work of writing her life, through the effort of which she was at last beginning to learn how intellect in honour and detachment might elucidate the clouded, terrible years.

Had Teresa been mystic only, it is likely that the austere peace of San José and the great effort of intellect and will exacted by the writing of her *Life* and of the superb, mystical works which were to follow it – *The Spiritual Relations*, *The Way of Perfection* and *The Interior Castle* – would have made up the rest of her earthly life; and the Church would still have had one of its most brilliant saints, and the world a woman of genius.

But she was also an ascetic, philosophically and practically; and looking with alarm upon her own day she saw that men, some men, could be and must be led back to the way of perfection through the ancient practices of the contemplative and ascetic life. She was, for the general, afraid of mysticism, and only examined it in writing under her vow of obedience, and protestingly. But the ascetic life she held to be within the reach of any serious person, and its usefulness and power comprehensible by all. So by degrees she came to see that not only had she to live it, she and a handful of disciples, in a small house in Avila, but that it was 'His Majesty's' will that she should re-establish it, preach it, re-present it throughout Spain, and the world; that she should challenge her superiors and the Mitigated Rule, and set up in contemporary society an Order of Carmel as nearly as possible the ancient one, and which she, at any rate, would know to be spiritually true.

There is not space here to set out the tactics, the ups and downs, or even broadly the strategy of her long war. But any who desire to learn its details will assuredly follow the campaign with zest if they read Mother Teresa's history of her Foundations, and with them, her Letters. More delicious letters have never been written – and the gay, vigorous, impatient, scampering and yet so saintly records of the Foundations are, if they were nothing else, a vibrant and non-stop entertainment.

Let those who will not have mysticism, for their own good or uncertain or bad reasons, be generous enough to a great fame, or even merely curious enough about it, to read these works I speak of. The saint's autobiography, and its beautiful *addenda*, spread out over her life, *The Spiritual Relations*, for all their lucidity, and their disarming will to communicate, to be simple and to make no vestige of false claim, may not be every man's reading: because their main purpose is to clarify a unique spiritual state. The two other major works of mysticism, *The Way of Perfection* and *The Interior Castle*, are, without a doubt, 'special' reading – to be pursued only by those who either are so truly attracted by Teresa's personality and purpose that, unworthy, unprepared, undeserving, they must read all she wrote; or, beyond those, if these writings fall into the hands of poets, or of the one or other who knows that God, and God only, is his pursuit – let him read, and move into the light that she will shed. For in these books the fearless and extended mystic speaks, the saint who can say in her spiritual maturity and physical decline that constantly in those busy years when she was in the midst of earthly affairs, when in conference about ways and means or about the conduct of this prioress or that novice, she was also in another place, in the presence of the Holy Trinity, and beholding, without a shadow of misunderstanding, the mystery of the Unity and Trinity. Authority, poetry and sublimity inform these works – therefore they are not for all markets and no sensible person will urge them on the man in the street.

But genius always has *something* to offer the man in

the street – otherwise, I think we may say, it would not be genius. And indeed I believe that Teresa, did she overhear me, would be horrified at my suggesting that she had not plenty.

Assuredly she had her humour, her irony, her common sense, and her deep, natural affections. She loved all the members of her own family with an exasperated fidelity which finds free expression in her letters and which must appeal to any member of any family. Her brothers, her sisters-in-law, her nieces – as we read her we grow concerned for them all. As she is, to the end. Still, she says more than once, as she struggles for the detachment of the true contemplative, that she finds it undesirable that her relations should visit her, that they upset and fuss her, and fill her with their preoccupations. Yet, to the end of her life all the members of her family could worry her – and also, she was very glad indeed to use the moneys her brother brought back from America for her foundation expenses.

She was, let us be emphatic – and let all who will say whatever they must say of 'levitations', 'transfixions' and the rest – the warmest, wittiest, most clear-eyed, most wilful and most pure of saint.

I suggest, uncertainly, that why she is so interesting is that she was not obviously endowed (except, by a freak, to the nor'west) for sainthood. She could have been any of about five perfectly good things – and made a mark in any of such directions. It happened that she heard, and went on hearing, 'His Majesty'. But had 'His Majesty' not caught her ear – and she will, I think, forgive me the irreverence – she would all the same have made her mark. She would have been a writer, anyway – which is something that few saints have been. And her writings, the simpler works no less than the profound, are a great gift she made to life.

The Foundation of San José in Avila was officially made, the first four sisters of the Reform receiving the habit and the Blessed Sacrament being placed in the little secretly prepared convent on St. Bartholomew's Feast, 24th August 1562. 'Well, it was like being in Heaven to me,' Teresa writes of that day's work.

Thereafter the remarkable news was out and 'commotion' of all kinds began outside St. Joseph's. Teresa, still a member of the community of El Encarnación and under 'obedience' to its Superior, was sent for at once, and had to leave her fledglings and go and be locked up in the great convent of the Mitigated for some days, to be questioned and lectured. 'I went in the belief that I should at once be put in prison. This, I think, would have been a great joy to me, as I should not have had to talk to anyone and should have been able to rest for a little and be alone.'

But she received no such respite. She had to talk; she had to fight.

No offence could be discovered in her audacious and guileful actio. Because she had so well and guilefully used the wits and good will of influential priests and laymen – we do not know exactly how – she had her patent and her brief from Rome. She had, we do not know why, the permission and blessing of the Bishop of Avila. She owned the little house, because of the love and generosity of her friend Doña Guiomár de Ulloa, who had been her hostess and shelter in three stormy years, and who was to end her days as one of her most devout Discalced. Now all that she and her companions asked to be allowed to do was to attempt to observe the rule of Mount Carmel without mitigation, in the form drawn up in 1247. So, although religious and civic authorities continued to fuss and argue, in an argument that Teresa would later cause to spread all through Spain, the Reform had begun, to the great content of the five nuns in San José.

The thirty-sixth chapter of the *Life* contains Teresa's clear, unaffected narration of the adventure of this first foundation, and is very entertainingly written; very gentle and happy in tone. 'The rule is rather strict, for meat is never eaten except in cases of necessity, there is an eight months' fast, and there are other ascetic practices, as may be seen in the primitive Rule. Yet many of these things seem to the sisters very light.'

And towards the end of the last chapter of the same work, chapter forty, she writes as follows:

'As I am now out of the world, and my companions are few and saintly, I look down upon the world as from above and care very little what people say or what is known about me. I care more about the smallest degree of progress achieved by one single soul than for all the things that people may say about me; for since I have been here it has been the Lord's will that this should become the aim of all my desires. He has given me a life which is a kind of sleep; when I see things I nearly always seem to be dreaming them. In myself I find no great propensity to joy or sorrow. If anything produces either of these conditions in me it passes so quickly that I marvel, and the feeling it leaves is like the feeling left by a dream.'

She had earned this tranquillity, and later was often to look back to it in wondering gratitude.

In the spring of 1567 the Father General of the Carmelite Order came from Rome to visit Spain. He inspected Teresa's small single convent of the Reform, and to her surprise approved of it, even to the extent of giving her patents for the foundation of other houses; later he also sent her licences to found, if she could, two monasteries of Reformed Carmelite monks. She was astonished, and inflamed to great zeal by this unlooked-for encouragement, which she may in part have owed to the King, Philip II, who was zealously advocating reform throughout all the religious orders at this time.

However, licences and congratulations were one thing; the means to proceed with 'His Majesty's' work against 'those Lutherans' were quite another. 'Here was a poor Discalced nun, without help from anywhere except from the Lord, loaded with patents and good wishes but devoid of all possibility of making them effective. But I was not devoid either of courage or of hope.'

She appealed for counsel to friends in the powerful Society of Jesus, at Medina del Campo. And very soon – in August of that year – 'without a house nor so much as a farthing for buying one' – she was on her way to that city with seven nuns, to attempt her second foundation.

Everyone in Avila, including her friend the Bishop, thought and said that this decision was mad. 'But I took little notice of them.' And, against such difficulties and obstacles as were, did she but know it, to crowd about her every future effort, she established her convent on Medina.

And there in the autumn, while pondering how she might ever set about her reform of the Carmelite monks, she met a small quiet young father of the Mitigated Rule, who was studying at Salamanca. He told her, as had already another Carmelite, Fray Antonio de Heredia, that he desired to live a more ascetic life, and was preparing to join the Carthusians. She begged him, as she had successfully begged the other, to await her plans, and that when she could find a monastery he could seek the way of perfection in his own Carmelite Order. He promised her that he would wait a little while. 'I liked him very much,' she wrote. And now that she had 'a monk and a half' to begin with, the thing seemed to her settled. The little 'half-monk' that she 'liked very much' was Fray Juan de la Cruz, St. John of the Cross.

The work was indeed on its way.

From Medina to Malagón, from Malagón to Valladolid; from Valladolid to Toledo, Pastrana, Salamanca. In the New Year of 1571, when she opened at Alba de Tormes the religious house in which she was to die, she had established within three and a half years nine convents of the Reform, and two monasteries.

She was fifty-two and a woman of very uncertain and difficult health when she left Avila for Medina, with everyone telling her she was mad. She had no money at all, and no security, and never would allow any of her convents to possess anything, or to rely on more than what 'His Majesty' would see to from day to day, as needs arose; she had the entire body of the Mitigated Rule in Spain actively opposed to her, and with it its many rich and influential friends in the hierarchy and the nobility; she was still very often a subject of scandal and gossip, and the Holy Office of the Inquisition still kept its cold eye on her. And she had to travel unceasingly about Castile, in all extremes of Castilian weather, and in conditions of hardship and discomfort which it is difficult for us to imagine now.

Fray Julián de Avila, her escort on most of her travels, has left us vivid accounts of them, and we can read of them also in Gracián's works. But they are best appreciated, because best and most racily described, in the *Book of Foundations* and in Teresa's Letters.

The Foundress and a little group of her nuns travelled on mules or donkeys, without saddles – she would have no such luxury – and accompanied by two or three friars of the Reform, as well as muleteers. The latter interested Teresa, and she disciplined them almost as if they were members of her Order. She allowed them no bad language, and taught them to respect all the conventual routine of her sisters as they travelled along. By the chime of the little bell, the religious day with its recitals of office, its periods of silence, meditation and recreation, was carried through on the mules' backs as in the cloister of San José. The muleteers learnt to respect and meticulously to supervise the nuns' privacy, so that in no matter what frightful inns they rested or slept, whatever else they had – vermin, broken roofs, infected water, pigs in their rooms with them – they had always that. And once Teresa had set out for any place, she did not turn back; no extreme of Castilian weather, no bad turn of her own bad health, no rumour that they would not welcome her where she was going, ever made her pause. It is recorded that on these roads she discoursed to her community of the highest spiritual themes – of the purposes of the ascetic life, of the value to the soul of obedience, of the methods of 'recollection', of the Prayer of Quiet and the Prayer of Union, as clearly and fluently as if she wrote. But in the hours of recreation she would make up poems and chants for them to sing, she would talk of daily concerns with passing peasants, who must have found her cavalcade a considerable novelty; and she would joke with the muleteers. And had these men been very good during the hours of prayer or silence she would find them something special to eat from the little store of dried fruits and suchlike that were carried along for emergencies.

And at the end of each of these journeys she had to go into battle. She hardly ever had a *duro* with which to begin a foundation. She made them all by backing up her extraordinary faith in God and her work with audacity second to no one's, a personal charm to which all her contemporaries testify and which rings in her books, and an unusually shrewd, cool brain.

So always she found a house of some kind, usually a tumbledown one, that someone would let her have, for 'His Majesty's' sake; always, by coaxing, writing, pestering, she contrived to have a little chapel made and consecrated, and the Blessed Sacrament brought to it, for no house was allowed to be a convent of hers until that had been done; always she found at least one or two young ladies of the neighbourhood clamouring to take the veil of the Discalced, having heard her legend, and this was very useful because it roused the interest of the neophytes' families, and usually brought alms or influence to the rescue of the cause. Always she found some pious aristocrat or some wealthy widow who fell under her spell and did her bidding. Always she found some learned doctor of the Church, or some respected Prior or Abbot to speak up for her – and nearly always she got round the Bishop of the place.

And, the little convent established in the poverty and uncertainty she insisted upon, her maximum complement of Prioress and twelve nuns settled in it, with 'His Majesty' in the tabernacle of their chapel and in charge of them, she would look for her mules and muleteers again, and with the three or four sisters hand-picked to begin the next foundation, she would be off on the road, to another battlefield. With the powers of the Mitigated Order thundering ever more angrily against her, with the Papal Nuncio abusing her in Madrid and in his despatches to Rome, with her own health tormenting her – but in perpetual serene conversation and argument with God, she rode off to wherever she decided next to promote 'His Majesty's' business.

As her work grew in influence so naturally grew the number of her enemies and censors in the Mitigated Order and among its powerful friends, in Rome as well as in Spain. It must be remembered that her Reform was not finally released from the jurisdiction of the Observance, that is the Chapter of the Mitigated, until 1581, the year before her death; so that she was working often in 'disobedience and contumacy', as a Papal Nuncio wrote of her, and always under unfriendly observation. Indeed every now and then she had temporarily to submit herself to very exacting instructions from the Carmelite Provincial. Once for instance, in October 1571, she was commanded back to her old convent of El Encarnación at Avila, as Prioress, and had to attempt to establish peace and order in that very turbulent house where she had lived for twenty-seven years.

She was successful in this difficult office which she held for three years, while still obstinately directing her Reform beyond the walls, visiting her Salamanca convent, directing her scattered Prioresses by letter, writing the *Book of Foundations*, and arranging her Segovia Foundation. And at last she was allowed to return to her beloved St. Joseph's, Avila, as Prioress, in October 1574. But during her period at El Encarnación Fray Juan de la Cruz was appointed confessor there. Her 'little half-monk' was now far advanced in the mystic life, and though by conscience and conviction an earnest pioneer of the Reform, an indomitable traveller, preacher and teacher – he was not, like Teresa, a man of action, but simply lived with God. Therefore for her in these very crowded days of her career, it was a delight to be able to discourse sometimes with one so sure of the one thing that truly mattered, love of God. It was a great refreshment, and must have compensated much for the irksomeness of having to govern a too-large convent by rules which she herself had long discarded.

In 1575 she carried her Discalced Rule south into Andalucia. She made three foundations there in that year, at Beas, at Sevilla and at Caravaca. She also welcomed home from the Spanish Indies two of the four dear brothers who had gone seeking their fortunes there. One of these brothers, Lorenzo, was especially dear to her, and his friendship and support was hers in everything henceforward, until his death in 1580.

In 1575 also she met Fray Jeronimo de la Madre de Dios, generally spoken of as Father Gracián.

This interesting and tragic man, a monk of the Reform, had recently been appointed by the Papal Nuncio as Provincial, subject to the Observance, of the Discalced friars and nuns of Spain. So on his election he came to Andalucia to present himself to

Mother Teresa. She was delighted with him. 'He pleased me so much that it seemed to me as if those who had praised him to me hardly knew him at all.'

He was young, eager, eloquent and cultured. Teresa regarded him as a woman of her age and knowledge might regard a brilliantly promising son. For the rest of her life she directed him, inspired him, worked him very hard, and fussed over him rather touchingly. And while she lived he was her most spectacular soldier of the Reform – perhaps her greatest. But after her death something went wrong for Gracián, and although John of the Cross fought valiantly for him, he could not or did not stay his course. His story darkened and saddened; he left Spain, left the Order, and disappeared into a wandering, uncertain life in Africa. That is, of course, another story. But often reading Teresa's letters one is compelled to wonder if she was as sure a judge of men as she was of women. Her enthusiasm for Gracián contrasts puzzlingly with her measured, not to say casual, appreciation of John of the Cross. But it is true that the former came to her at a time when her cause needed a man of the world, a man of action – and Gracián was such, and she knew it.

Thereafter, from their meeting and the Sevilla foundation, battle was really joined, at top level as we would say now, for this issue of Mitigated or Reformed Rule. The Fathers Provincial, and the Mothers Superior, of the Observance went fiercely into action in 1575, to put a stop to Teresa's work. Rome, the King, the Nuncio, all the Bishops of Spain were compelled to take sides, or to seem to do so. Chapters-General of the Order were held again and again, to adopt harsh measures against the Reformers. Gracián, John of the Cross and other Discalced monks were arrested, released, arrested again by the Fathers of the Observance. Teresa wrote her usual cool protests to the King, the Cardinal, the Nuncio; but meantime she was also subject to the cat-and-mouse tactics of her superiors, and was forbidden to go here, to go there, to write this, that and the other. It was useless however to issue laws to her. She heard only one authoritative voice, 'His Majesty's' and whatever that told her to do she did. Whenever that voice told her to have patience – as often it did – she struggled to have patience. No earthly monitor could now, however, arouse that virtue in her. And wherever she was, as long as there were goose-quills to be had – and she said that the only good ones came from Avila – she continued to write. Not only her letters, her records, her contributions and instructions; not only her little songs and poems to amuse her nuns and, as she said, to indulge her own vanity; but also, through these years of real, dangerous battle with powers that truly could destroy her life-work, she wrote her two greatest mystical works, *The Way of Perfection* and *The Interior Castle*.

Also, throughout the confusion, she went placidly on with her foundations. After Caravaca, Villanueva. And in the year of her brother's death, grieving and ill and feeling often in that autumn of 1580 a great loneliness, and many spiritual and temporal fears for herself and all her charges, she came to Palencia and founded a convent there in the last week of the cold, sad year.

But triumph, political triumph at least, was at hand. Teresa probably owed more to Philip II than is clearly known. She wrote to him often, and succinctly. There is an unproven legend that she once interviewed him in Madrid. If she did it is sad that we have no record of their meeting; but since we have no word of it from her the suggestion is almost certainly apocryphal. But we do know that he favoured reform of the religious houses, and favoured Teresa's work; and although he was a man of infinite circuitousness of thought and action, he also had some skill with clerics and politicians, and frequently got his own way, without seeming to have strained overmuch for it.

Therefore, it is not surprising to find his subtle authority behind the events of 3rd March 1581, when at the Chapter of Alcalá de Henares the Discalced Carmelites, friars and nuns, were finally released from the authority of the Mitigated Order, and committed to the government of Father Gracián. 'Which was all that we desired', wrote Teresa, 'for our peace and quietness. On the petition of our Catholic King, Don Philip, a brief conferring amplest powers to this effect was obtained from Rome... The King bore the cost of it [the Chapter at Alcalá] and at his command the whole University helped us... this proved to be one of the most joyful and satisfying experiences that I could ever have in this life... Now, Calced and Discalced alike, we are all at peace, and no one hinders us in Our Lord's service.'

Ourwardly, the work was done. There were to be yet the foundations of Soria, Granada and Burgos – Burgos perhaps almost the most severe of all her travels and battles. But in April, her last earthly April, that too was safe and established, and the sick, tired woman could mount her mule and ride to Avila.

It seems a pity that she could not stay there, rest there, through that summer. She should have died in

Avila. But she had to work her way to death. During the summer she visited her convents at Palencia, Valladolid and Medina del Campo. In September she was very ill, but her Provincial commanded her to go to Alba de Tormes. She was dying when she got there at the end of the month.

From her cell she could see, when they propped her up, the flowing Tormes river. Water, the movements and changes of water, had always attracted her, and been a chief symbol, a chief source of exposition for her of the movements and developments of prayer. As she watched the river now, beyond the garden and through the few, slim, rustling willow-trees, doubtless she prayed more successfully than ever; doubtless she had no anxiety now in accomplishing with will and intellect the Prayer of Union.

She may have been lonely for Avila of her childhood, and known that she would not see its towers and walls again. But it is not far from Alba – she would have thought nothing of that mule-ride. And the Salamancan landscape that her dying eyes received was gold and tawny in those September days as was the high *paramera* of home; and the sky was Castile's immaculate blue, that she had known and suffered under in sixty-seven years. She was not far from home in those last hours, if she still acknowledged in her affectionate but purified heart that earthly word. But she was a saint and had spoken for years with God. So who is to guess what memories or none she had as she waited for 'His Majesty' and watched the riverwater running by?

She died on 4th October 1582. She died repeating *'Cor contritum et humiliatum Deus non despicies.'*

This has been an attempt to present the great saint in her human aspect, in her personal appeal to one very far removed from understanding of saintliness. And now I have written all the words I may, and I know that I have failed to do the simple-seeming thing I attempted. It is no good. The great, the illuminated, the chosen ones, even while they are of our flesh and to that extent share our dangers and humiliations, yet so translate those threats, so dazzlingly purify them that they are not to be interpreted by our poor rushlights of surmise. Teresa was made of flesh like us, and that it plagued and wearied her – in youth, through its energetic, natural storms, and in maturity and age through its infirm, sick drag on her spirit – we know. But after that? We can read her indeed, and learn and wonder – but what comment dare we make on a fellow creature who has sped so far while seeming to stay with us? Crashaw can snatch great phrases for Teresa's 'draughts of intellectual day', but she escapes him, as, the more one reads her, the more one understands she must escape us all. Probably it was all that she desired to do, apart from pleasing 'His Majesty' and doing what He told her.

Yet the human charm persists, and we persist in twisting it over and puzzling at it; because its humanity relates the great one to us, and that is not only flattering but also consoling.

Teresa was a saint. She was alarming, she was, if you like, deluded; she was, if you like, mad. But she accomplished a great deal, speaking mundanely; she wrote with sanity, beauty and modesty, about high and dangerous matters; she charmed almost everyone she ever met; she was gay, tender and witty in her letters and in all her writings, and she was as much impeded by small faults and vanities as any saint dare be – as well she knew. So, however far beyond us she extended here on earth, she still is ours and dear to us, in a large part of her records. She was indeed Teresa of Jesus, as 'His Majesty' told her; but still somehow we cling to her in hope. She was once a sinner, as she is never tired of telling us; she was always a wit and an observer; she loved her brothers and her friends. Dangerous as her territory may be we do not find it barren of the flowers we know. The trouble really is that, incomprehensible as she may finally be, no sane person can read Teresa without liking her. The charm lives with the sanctity, the wit with the vision, the human simplicity with the ineffable raptures.

'You must forgive me,' she would write to a friend she had hurt. 'With those I love I am insufferable, so anxious am I to have them perfect in everything.'

To 'His Majesty' she often complained of His harsh treatment. Once, when He had tried her almost past her strength she grumbled very firmly, and heard Him reply: 'Teresa, this is how I treat My friends.' 'Which is why You have so few,' said she.

On another occasion she was importuning Him unmercifully, night and day, in regard to the insuperable-seeming difficulties of her Burgos foundation – when she heard Him say: 'I have heard you, daughter. Please leave Me alone.' Whereat, she records, she was as much delighted and reassured as if the convent was already happily established. (She had an endearing way of reporting 'His Majesty' as if He spoke very much in her own forthright style.)

To find the full charm of her one must read her letters – to her prioresses, to Gracián, to her spiritual directors. 'I laughed at what you told me...' '...Ah, how I have been amused!' And when she has narrated some comedy or quoted some light poem of her own: 'God forgive you,' she writes, 'for making me waste my time like this!'

She was nimble at occasional verse, and vain of her skill in this *genre*. Among her many attempts none is more amusing than the hymn she wrote for her community when they were afraid that their new, poor habits, of very coarse frieze, were likely to attract and harbour vermin.

> *Since Thou givest us, King of Heaven,*
> *New clothes like these,*
> *Do Thou keep all nasty creatures*
> *Out of this frieze.*
> *Daughters, you've the Cross upon you;*
> *Have courage too.*
> *Since salvation He has won you,*
> *He'll bring you through.*
> *He'll direct you, He'll defend you,*
> *If Him you please.*

ALL: *Do Thou keep all nasty creatures*
*Out of this frieze!*

There are more verses, with the same refrain. Teresa and her nuns at St. Joseph's, Avila, sang this composition in choir on the first day of their anxiety about the new habits – which shows that life was not without gaiety in her houses. Indeed it was not. She had a resounding way with ordinary life. We have all surely heard her famous claim for commonplace labours: *Entre los pucheros anda el Señor*. 'The Lord walks among the saucepans.'

She was brilliant herself among the saucepans – the best cook in the Order, her contemporaries said. And an undaunted scrubber of floors and washer and mender of clothes. A full and ordinary human being, in fact; one actively and truly with her fellows, though always ahead of them too, and by an accident in regard to which she was always reticent, above them.

'Whence He comes and how, she cannot tell, but so it is, and for as long as it lasts she cannot cease to be aware of the fact. When the vision leaves her, she cannot recall it to the imagination, however much she may wish to do so; for clearly, if she could, it would be a case of imagination and not of actual presence, to recapture which is not in her power; and so it is with all supernatural matters. And it is for this reason that the person to whom God grants this favour has no esteem for himself. He sees that it is a free gift and that he can neither add to it nor subtract from it.'